THE STARS OF
THE
HUNGER
GAMES
INSIDE OUT Unauthorised

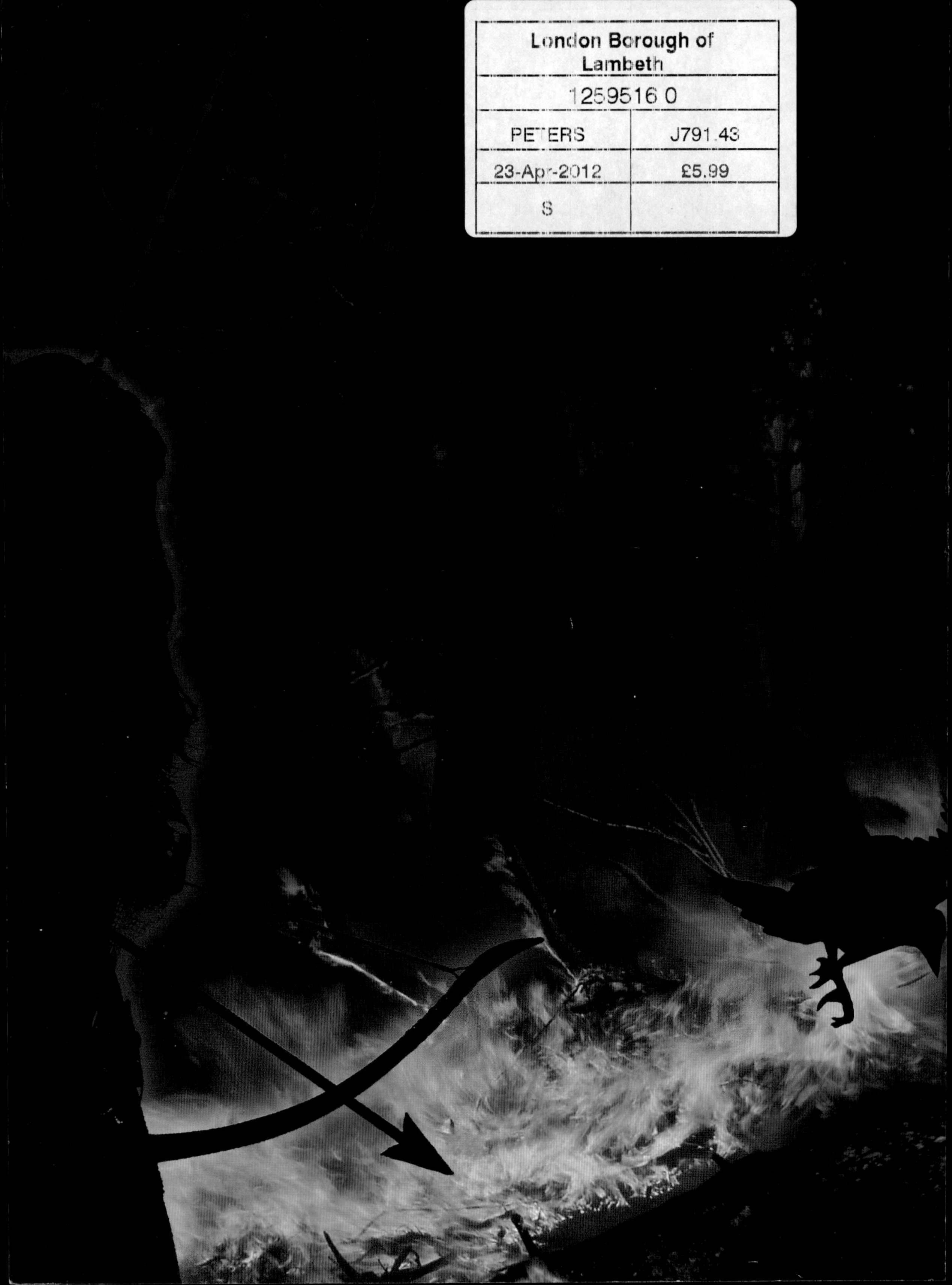

THE STARS OF

THE HUNGER GAMES

INSIDE OUT Unauthorised

MEL WILLIAMS

PICCADILLY PRESS • LONDON

May the Odds Be Ever in Your Favour!

Imagine the future, where the nation of Panem lies in the ruins of North America. A shining city called the Capitol – a place of plenty – is surrounded by twelve poverty-stricken districts in which the inhabitants struggle to survive. Every year, the Capitol demands that each district sends one girl and one boy to take part in a brutal Big Brother-style reality TV show – the Hunger Games. Twenty-four children are forced to enter the arena. But only the winner survives . . .

Portraying these incredible characters are the next young movie megastars! Joining Kristen Stewart, Robert Pattinson and Taylor Lautner in the Hollywood hall of fame will be Jennifer Lawrence, Josh Hutcherson and Liam Hemsworth, who play the captivating main characters in *The Hunger Games* blockbuster film. But is Jennifer really an archery ace like her character, Katniss? Is Josh as artistic as his alter-ego, Peeta? And is Liam in love with Jen in real life? This book will tell you what these screen sensations are really like, inside and out.

GIRL on *fire*

Meet Katniss Everdeen

Katniss Everdeen is too busy helping her depressed mother and young sister Prim survive the harsh coal-mining conditions of District 12 to realise how beautiful and courageous she is. However, she has captured the hearts of both her trusted friend, Gale Hawthorne, and local baker's boy, Peeta Mellark.

When her younger sister is chosen to be District 12's female tribute in the Hunger Games, Katniss immediately volunteers to take her place. In the arena, Katniss is forced to choose between love and life . . .

Many young, upcoming actresses were desperate to play Katniss. After auditions were held and Jennifer Lawrence was chosen, the novel's author, Suzanne Collins, said: "I felt there was only one who truly captured the character I wrote in the book. Jennifer's just an incredible actress . . ."

Fast fact . . .

Jennifer has never had an acting lesson. She just relies on her instincts.

Quick quiz

Q) Katniss's father taught her survival skills such as hunting. What happened to him?

A) He was killed in a mining accident when she was eleven.

Jennifer Lawrence's
CREDENTIALS

Full name: Jennifer Shrader Lawrence

Nickname: Jen

Birthdate: 15 August 1990

Born: Louisville, Kentucky, USA

Height: 1.7 metres (5 feet 7 inches)

Family: Jennifer's father, Gary, once owned a concrete construction firm. He now runs a children's camp called Camp Hi Ho, with her mother, Karen. Jennifer has two older brothers – Ben and Blaine.

Start in acting: Jennifer began acting in church plays. She decided at fourteen that she wanted to be an actress. Her mum took her to a talent agency in New York City who said she was the best fourteen year old they had ever seen. She modelled and appeared in commercials before winning parts in TV shows and movies. She now lives in Santa Monica, California.

Hobbies: Jennifer relaxes by playing guitar.

Fast fact
Jennifer played blue
mutant Mystique in
X-Men: First Class.
It took seven
people eight hours
to get her made up
and into costume.

Jen's tribute talents

Katniss is sixteen years old, dark-haired and olive-skinned.

Jennifer is in her early twenties, blonde and pale – but she has the right maturity to be convincing as a teenage rebel, and costume and hair stylists helped her get into character.

Katniss has excellent survival and hunting skills.

Jennifer is rough and tough too. For various movie roles, she's had to learn how to chop wood, handle guns and skin a squirrel, as well as undergoing gruelling physical training, including combat, rock climbing and archery.

When Katniss becomes a tribute she is thrust into the limelight and groomed in the Capitol as a celebrity.

Jen knows what it's like to become suddenly very famous. "I have hair and make-up people coming to my house every day and putting me in new, uncomfortable, weird dresses and expensive shoes, and I just shut down and raise my arms up for them to get the dress on, and pout my lips when they need to put the lipstick on. That's exactly what it's like for Katniss."

Katniss has a steely determination to get through any situation she finds herself in.

Jen has said: "I like when things are hard; I'm very competitive. If something seems difficult or impossible, it interests me."

Jen Says . . .

"I love that this [is a] look at our world that's obsessed with reality TV and with brutality . . . There are these scenes where it honestly looks like gladiators [from] Roman history: people murdering other people for nothing more than entertainment . . . All of that is genius and hard hitting and fascinating."

Fast fact . . .

Jennifer graduated from high school two years early, by studying online, in order to pursue acting.

"I've just always loved stories, in any way, shape or form: TV, movies, books, writing. If I was in the car, and I had no way to any of those things, my parents had to tell me one story after another after another. So now I get to tell stories for the rest of my life."

The Boy with the Bread

Meet Peeta Mellark

Katniss Everdeen's family are so poor that they faced starvation. Peeta Mellark is the son of the baker in District 12 – his family are better off, although they still cannot afford to eat the bread, buns and cakes they bake unless they are stale leftovers. Katniss has no idea that Peeta is in love with her until he reveals it in a TV interview. Even then, she thinks it is a Hunger Games strategy. However, Peeta proves it in the arena by trying to protect her – something he first did when they were little: he saw Katniss rummaging through rubbish for food and gave her two loaves of bread, despite knowing he would be beaten for it. Peeta is valiant, steadfast and true to himself, and is determined to show the Capitol that they don't own him, that he is more than just a piece in their games . . .

The movie's director, Gary Ross, said: "I thought Peeta would be the hardest role to cast, and I feel so lucky that we found someone who embodies every aspect of such a complex character." This talented young actor is Josh Hutcherson.

Fast fact . . .

Josh's all-time hero is Batman.

Quick quiz

Q) From what age did Peeta have a crush on Katniss?

A) He noticed her on their first day of school, when they were just five.

Fast fact . . .

Josh has worked with Hollywood megastars including Tom Hanks, in *The Polar Express*, Robin Williams, in *RV*, and Brendan Fraser, in *Journey to the Centre of the Earth*.

Josh Hutcherson's
CREDENTIALS

Full name: Joshua Ryan Hutcherson

Birthdate: 12 October 1992

Born: Union, Kentucky, USA

Height: 1.7 metres (5 feet 7 inches)

Family: Mother – Michelle, who is now employed as his personal assistant. Father – Chris, who works for the USA Environmental Protection Agency. Younger brother – Connor, who also acts. Josh is very close to his family.

Pets: A puppy named Diesel, a dog named Baxter, two cats, Jell-O and Paws, and some fish.

Start in acting: Josh decided when he was four that he wanted to be an actor. His parents weren't keen, but by the age of nine he had begged them so much to let him try that they got him a local agent. He then got an acting coach, went to California for some auditions and began to win roles. Josh's inspiration is movie star Jake Gyllenhaal.

Hobbies: Josh enjoys all sports, from soccer to bowling. He also loves cars and motorbikes.

Josh's tribute talents

Peeta is sixteen years old, with ash-blond hair and blue eyes. He is fit and muscular from spending his childhood heaving sacks of flour. Josh is naturally dark-haired but went blond for the movie. He trained hard for the role and put on fifteen pounds of muscle in three weeks.

Peeta is in love with Katniss, even when she is cold to him.

Josh said in a magazine interview:

"I feel like every relationship I get into ends up being like that! I am someone who can fall in love at the drop of a hat."

He has dated *High School Musical* star Vanessa Hudgens but says that his celebrity crush is Zoe Saldana of *Avatar* and *Star Trek*.

In the arena, Peeta's special skill is camouflage. Josh loves all outdoor pursuits and is good at rock climbing, mountain biking and cliff-diving. He even competes in triathlons – extremely tough races involving swimming, biking and running long distances.

Josh Says . . .

"Imagination is such an important part in everybody's life . . . I think that is kind of lost a lot in kids because they play so many video games. I was always raised outside, playing and imagining and making up games."

"I like girls I can have deep conversations with — the meaning of life and existence . . ."

Jen on Josh:

"Josh is so charming . . . he's sweet, he's down to earth, he's normal. He embodies all of it and brings it all to Peeta."

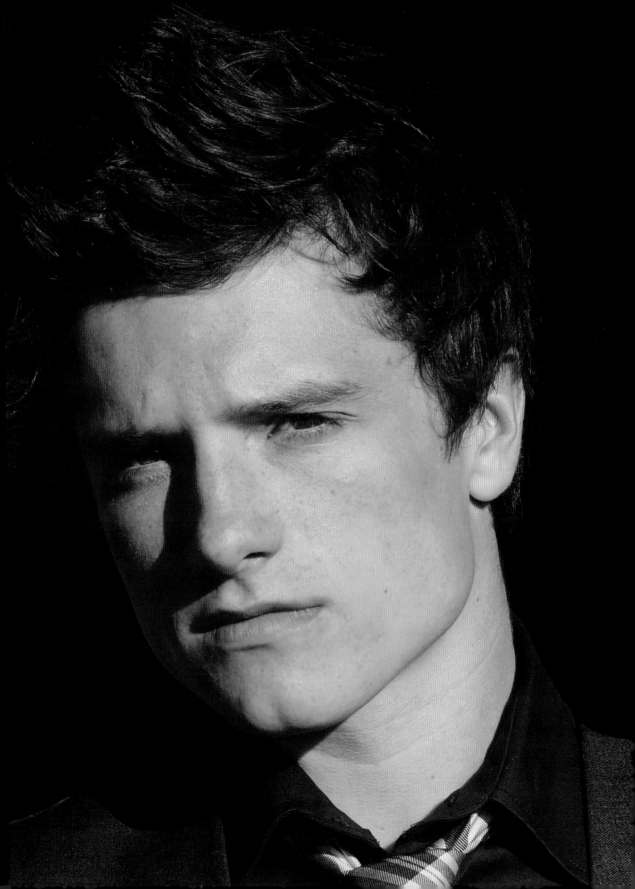

The Boy with the Bow

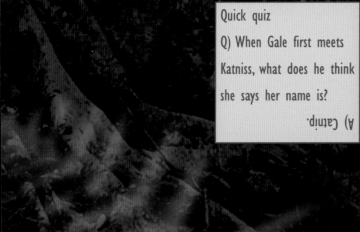

Quick quiz

Q) When Gale first meets Katniss, what does he think she says her name is?

A) Catnip.

23

Liam Hemsworth's
CREDENTIALS

Full name: Liam Hemsworth

Birthdate: 13 January 1990

Born: Melbourne, Australia

Height: 1.91 metres (6 feet 3 inches)

Family: Mother – Leonie, father – Craig, and two older brothers – Chris and Luke, who are both actors.

Start in acting: Liam began to follow in his brothers' footsteps in high school, when he took on an agent. He was sixteen when he went to his first audition. From 2007 he began to appear on TV shows including *Home and Away* and *Neighbours*. In March 2009, Liam moved to the States to try out for movies. He won his first film role when he had been in Los Angeles for only three weeks and had not yet even found an agent there . . . Liam's favourite actors are Matt Damon, Leonardo DiCaprio and Will Smith.

Hobbies: As a teenager, Liam's family moved to Phillip Island, a small beach town, where he became a keen surfer. Liam has said: "When I was at school, that's all that pretty much mattered in my life."

Liam's rebel talents

Gale has olive skin, straight black hair and grey eyes, and is very tall. Katniss describes him as being so good looking that he could have any girl he wants. Tall and handsome, Liam has the perfect looks to play Gale (with a little help to dye his blond hair). His first leading role in a movie was opposite Miley Cyrus in *The Last Song* – she couldn't resist his charms and fell in love with him!

Gale wants passionately to fight back against the evil Capitol, but because of the possible consequences for his friends and family, he has to bite his lip and live with it.

Liam and his family have always been strong supporters of just causes – both his parents are child protection workers. But Liam has said that, like Gale, "I've definitely had times where I've had to hold back what I really want to say or do."

Gale and Peeta are rivals for Katniss's affections. Liam Hemsworth and Josh Hutcherson got on brilliantly during their six weeks together on set – so well that Liam has said: "Peeta and Gale are actually best friends in real life."

Fast fact . . .

Details magazine selected Liam as one of their predictions for *The Next Generation of Hollywood's Leading Men*.

Liam Says . . .

"I want to do things that I'm genuinely interested in and believe in. I want to make good stories!"

"I love getting into physical shape for a film – it makes me feel more like the character needs to be."

> ## Fast fact . . .
> Liam lost out on the role of leading man in the movie *Thor* to his older brother, Chris.

Jen on Liam:
"Liam is a solid brick of muscle . . .
but he's got depth and he's interesting and
at the same time he's natural and he flows."

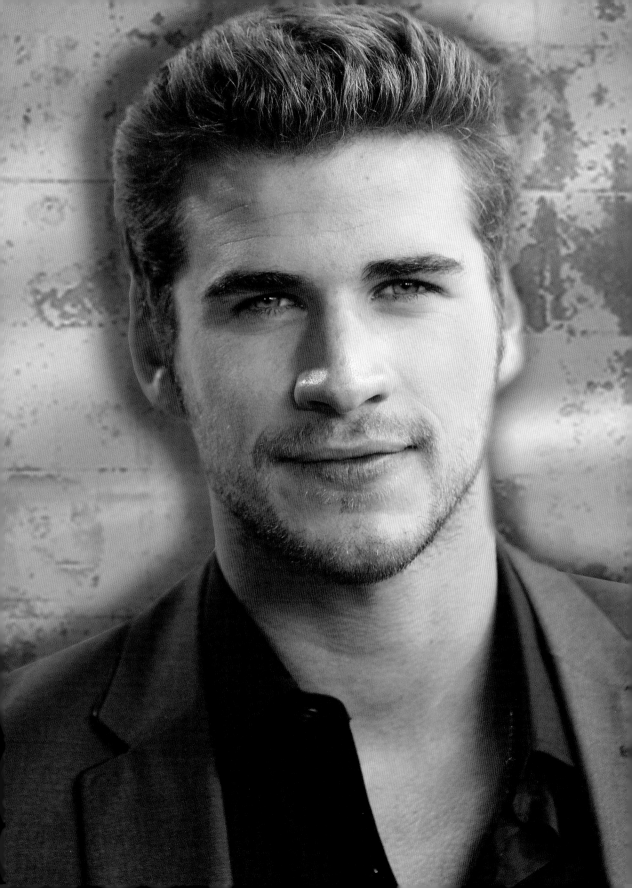

Meet Cato

Fast fact . . .

Alexander got through 16 auditions to land the lead role in the movie, *The Dark is Rising*.

Katniss describes Cato as a monster from District 2. Cato is one of the Career Tributes – boys and girls who come from wealthier districts than Katniss's, where they have been trained and fed especially to compete in the Hunger Games and are ruthless killing machines in the arena. Cato becomes Katniss's sworn enemy from the moment she scores higher than him in training. He later tells the other Career Tributes that he wants to be the one to kill her, in his own way – and that's how he feels even *before* she blows up his cache of supplies ...

Who could be more perfect to play Cato than Alexander Ludwig – a guy who played a lead role fighting alien assassins in Disney's *Race to Witch Mountain*.

Full name:	Alexander Richard Ludwig
Birthdate:	7 May 1992
Born:	Vancouver, Canada
Height:	1.83 metres (6 foot)
Family:	Alexander has three younger siblings. His father, Harald, is a businessman, and his mother, Sharlene, a former actress.
Start in acting:	Alexander began acting when he was nine, in a Harry Potter toy advert. He then signed with an agent and began landing movie and TV roles.
Hobbies:	Alexander is an avid athlete. He surfs, water skiis, and plays tennis, basketball and ice hockey.

Tribute talents
Cato has a ruthless temper when he loses.
Alexander is also hugely competitive.
He loves taking part in extreme freestyle ski
competitions on Whistler Mountain.

Meet Clove

Clove is Cato's counterpart from District 2 – and Katniss's most dreaded female rival. She is a vicious, bloodthirsty girl who is the first to make a kill when she throws a knife into the District 9 boy tribute's back in the opening seconds of the games. Katniss is nearly next, but fortune is on her side when Clove's second knife throw finds only her backpack, not her back. Katniss has a second lucky escape when Clove is on the point of cutting up her in order to give the audience a show.

This challenging role is played by fourteen-year-old Isabelle Fuhrman.

Full name:	Isabelle Fuhrman
Birthdate:	25 February 1997
Born:	Washington, D.C., USA. Raised in Atlanta, Georgia.
Family:	Isabelle's Soviet-born mother, Elina, is a journalist and her father, Nick, is in politics and business. Older sister, Madeline, is a singer-songwriter.
Start in acting:	Isabelle was seven when she began acting character voices on the Cartoon Network. She then performed in adverts, before winning parts in theatre and TV shows like *Ghost Whisperer*. At eleven, Isabelle went into movies.
Hobbies:	Isabelle enjoys playing guitar and singing. She also loves animals. She has two dogs (Lilly and Jennings) and had a hamster named Lola that she carried around everywhere until it sadly died in 2009.

Tribute talents

Clove delights in blood, pain and death.

Isabelle starred in horror flick *Orphan* as an extremely violent serial killer.

Quick quiz

Q) At the "feast", one of Katniss's arrows hits which part of Clove's body?

A) Her upper left arm. Unfortunately for Katniss, Clove throws knives with her right . . .

Fast fact . . .

Isabelle is playing the lead in the movie remake of the classic novel, *A Little Princess*, as the brave, sweet character Sara Crewe — totally opposite from evil Clove!

Meet Thresh

The male tribute from District 11 is Thresh, a huge hulking boy who keeps himself to himself. He hardly ever speaks, and when he does, he only mutters. He shows little interest in training, where Katniss describes him as a giant: probably six and a half feet tall, and built like an ox. To her amazement, in the arena she thinks he gains weight and becomes even more massive and powerful. Thresh can be violent and brutal, but he also has a strong sense of honour. Thresh is played by Hollywood newcomer, Dayo Okeniyi.

Full name:	Oladayo A. Okeniyi (Oladayo means "our wealth has become joy")
Birthdate:	14 June 1988
Born:	Lagos, Nigeria. He moved with his family to the USA in 2003.
Family:	Dayo is the youngest of five siblings. His father is a retired customs officer. His mother is a British literature teacher.
Start in acting:	Dayo became interested in theatre at elementary school. He studied at university for a degree in visual communications design, then moved to Los Angeles to try to become an actor.
Hobbies:	Dayo enjoys hip hop dancing, singing, and sports such as soccer, American football, swimming and rollerblading.

Tribute talents

In the arena, Thresh protects himself by lurking in a sinister field of shoulder-high grass, where Katniss and Peeta imagine there might be dangerous, hidden terrors.

Before landing the part of Thresh, Dayo played the lead in a horror movie set in the midst of a wild, terrifying forest.

Dayo is skilled at languages — he speaks fluent Yoruba and French, besides English.

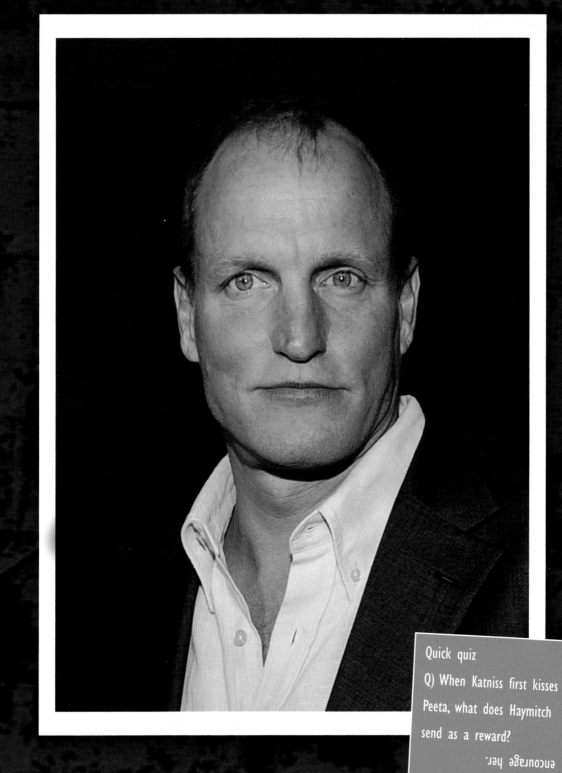

Quick quiz

Q) When Katniss first kisses Peeta, what does Haymitch send as a reward?

A) A pot of hot broth to encourage her.

Meet Haymitch Abernathy

In 74 years of Hunger Games, District 12 has had just two winners. Only one is still alive: Haymitch Abernathy. He has become a paunchy, middle-aged alcoholic, who has the depressing job each year of mentoring the two new District 12 tributes, who invariably die. From the moment at the reaping when Haymitch topples off the stage drunk, Katniss and Peeta have a very low opinion of him. However, he doesn't think much of them either – until they finally snap and vent their anger at him. Their spirit sparks his interest and hope, and he begins to give them advice and help which prove invaluable in the arena. Haymitch is a character you either love or loathe. He is portrayed by veteran Hollywood star, Woody Harrelson.

Full name:	Woodrow Tracy Harrelson
Birthdate:	23 July 1961
Born:	Midland, Texas
Start in acting:	Woody studied theatre arts and English at college, then moved to New York to try acting. He began in theatre, then got his big break playing a bartender in a hugely popular TV sitcom called *Cheers* for eight years. During this time he also began to star in movies.
Hobbies:	Woody is passionate about green issues and attends festivals and protests in support of saving the planet.

Mentor talents
Haymitch knows what appeals to an audience and advises Katniss and Peeta on how they should act, in order to win essential supplies from sponsors. Woody is so skilled at acting that he has won many important awards, including two nominations for Hollywood's top award, an Oscar.

Effie Trinket works as a chaperone for the District 12 Hunger Games tributes – from drawing their names at the reaping to escorting them to and around the Capitol. Effie is bubbly and breezy and insists on good manners in all situations – she seems totally oblivious to the plight of the tributes, although perhaps this is just part of her determination to keep up appearances. At first, Effie longs to be promoted from District 12 to a wealthier, more prestigious district. But as time goes by she warms to Katniss and Peeta and seems genuinely to care for them. Overenthusiastic Effie is played by Elizabeth Banks.

Full name:	Elizabeth Maresal Mitchell (Elizabeth Banks is her stage name)
Birthdate:	10 February 1974
Born:	Massachusetts, USA
Start in acting:	As a school girl, Elizabeth loved riding horses and other sports. After breaking her leg playing baseball, she tried something calmer – the school play. From then on, she was hooked on acting. She studied theatre at university and began appearing in movies.
Hobbies:	Elizabeth and her husband both enjoy fantasy football! She also loves horror films – her two favourites are *Poltergeist* and *Alien*.

Chaperone talents

Effie comes from the Capitol, where grooming, good looks and fashion are all important.

Elizabeth is a spokeswoman for L'Oreal beauty products.

Meet Effie Trinket

Quick quiz

Q) At the District 12 reaping, what is Effie's hair like?

A) She wears a pink, curly wig.

Meet Cinna

Katniss stuns the audience as the "girl on fire", all due to her stylist in the Capitol, Cinna. Cinna dresses Katniss in daring, breathtaking designs which use the showbiz glamour surrounding the Games to reveal their barbaric core. This is daring, rebellious and dangerous – and the audience love it! Cinna's own personal style is understated and subtle – totally opposite to the other Capitol fashionistas, who follow absurd trends in hair, make-up and cosmetic surgery. Cinna is played by music legend, Lenny Kravitz.

Full name:	Leonard Albert Kravitzovich (Lenny Kravitz is a stage name)
Birthdate:	26 May 1964
Born:	New York City, USA. At age ten, he moved with his family to Los Angeles.
Start in performing:	Lenny knew from the age of five that he wanted to be a musician and his parents, who were both in TV, encouraged him. Lenny began performing his own music at sixteen and recording at eighteen. He went on to become a major rock star and win countless awards. In 2001 Lenny appeared in the feature film *Zoolander*. He starred in three other movies as himself before taking on his first acting role in 2009 in a hard-hitting drama called *Precious*.

Stylist credentials
Cinna can see Katniss's true nature and designs costumes for her which reflect this. He becomes Katniss's trusted friend.
Lenny has said: "I identify with women more than men. I guess I have a strong feminine side."

Fast fact . . .

Lenny is also a music producer who has worked with both Michael Jackson and Madonna.

Meet Rue

Twelve-year-old Rue is the small, slight girl tribute from the orchards of District 12. Back home, Rue supports her younger siblings, risking her life to forage in the meadows for food. She is daring and has a spirit for adventure. Katniss used to enjoy singing with her father, and music is what Rue loves most in all the world – she can even communicate by singing with birds called mockingjays.

Full name:	Amandla Stenberg (Amandla means "power" in Zulu)
Birthdate:	23 October 1998
Born:	Los Angeles, California
Height:	A tiny 1.42 metres (4 feet 8 inches)
Family:	Amandla's mother is African-American and her father is Danish.
Start in acting:	Amandla started modelling at four, and acting shortly afterwards, doing adverts and voiceovers. She won her first film role in 2010.

Tribute talents

Rue's special skill is moving lightly from tree to tree, undetected.
Amandla has trained in the nimble sport of free-running.

Rue is very musical, and can even get the mockingjays to sing with her.
Amandla plays violin, drums and guitar in a band.

Quick quiz

Q) When Katniss's enemies spot her up a tree, Rue suggests an escape. What is this?

A) Rue points out a deadly trackerjacker nest that Katniss can drop on them.

Meet Caesar Flickerman

Caesar Flickerman is the face of the Hunger Games TV show.
When interviewing the tributes, he is skilled at bringing out
their personalities to entertain and dazzle the audience.
He is played in the movie by the talented Stanley Tucci.

Full name:	Stanley Tucci
Birthdate:	11 November 1960
Born:	Peekskill, New York, USA
Start in acting:	Stanley has loved acting since his high school drama club. He has has appeared in countless theatre and TV shows and movies, and won many awards.

Showbiz talents

Caesar Flickerman likes to look good. He changes the colour of his hair, eyelids
and lips for each Hunger Games that he presents.

**Stanley is renowned for changing his voice, hair and other physical attributes
for the sake of the film characters he plays.**

Citizens of the Capitol, like Caesar, are very concerned
with their appearance and living an opulent lifestyle.

**Stanley appeared in fashion movie *The Devil Wears
Prada* and has said: "I love clothes. I love to go
shopping. I love to be fussed over . . ."**

Fast fact . . .
Caesar Flickerman has
hosted the Hunger Games
interviews for over
40 years.

Meet Prim

Primrose Everdeen is the younger sister of Katniss, and was the female tribute from District 12 chosen at random to take part in the Hunger Games. But Katniss can't bear the thought of her little sister in the arena. Even with her natural instinct for healing, Prim is timid and compassionate, and Katniss knows she would certainly be killed. To protect her, Katniss volunteers to take her place in the Hunger Games. Actress Willow Shields brings her to life in the movie.

Full name:	Willow Shields
Birthdate:	1 June 2000
Born:	Albuquerque, New Mexico, USA
Family:	Willow's twin sister, Autumn, and older brother, River, are also actors.
Start in acting:	Willow has been acting since 2008. She has appeared on a TV show *In Plain Sight* and in a movie called *Beyond the Blackboard*.

Tribute talents

Prim is good with animals and has a farm goat and a cat to look after.
Willow loves animals too, especially her pet dogs. She also keeps chickens!

To survive in District 12, Prim must make the most of what she finds around her.
Willow's hobbies include getting creative with arts and crafts.

Director Gary Ross says . . .

"Prim is an emotionally demanding role and in many ways she is the cornerstone of the story."

Meet President Coriolanus Snow

The cruel, ruthless leader of the nation of Panem, President Snow is ultimately in control of the Hunger Games, and the lives of the tributes. He is played by Hollywood legend Donald Sutherland.

Full name:	Donald Sutherland
Birthdate:	17 July 1935
Born:	New Brunswick, Canada
Start in acting:	Donald began performing at fourteen as a radio announcer. He studied engineering and drama at university, then worked on stage and TV in Britain before moving to Hollywood. He has starred in movies as heroes and villains for over forty years. He even has a star on the Hollywood Walk of Fame.

Villainous talents

President Snow is a chilling figure with "snake eyes" who is intimidating even when he is smiling.

Donald is excellent at playing ruthless, cruel baddies. He played such a terrifying leader in a movie called *1990* that he couldn't bring himself to watch the finished film for years.

A private and cunning manipulator, Snow is described as a thin and unassumingly small man.

Donald is 1.93 metres (6 feet 4 inches) tall, and known for being very friendly – he makes an effort to remember everyone's names in a film crew when he's working on a movie.

A worldwide phenomenon . . .

The Hunger Games novel has had astounding success. It has hit bestseller lists all around the world and millions of copies have been sold in over 44 countries — more than 5.4 million copies in the USA alone! *The Hunger Games* movie is expected to have equally record-breaking success. Experts have predicted that it will be even bigger than vampire blockbuster *Twilight*, which has grossed over $392 million!

Quick quiz

Q) How much did *The Hunger Games* movie cost to make?

A) Just under $100 million.

Director Gary Ross says . . .

"As much as the firestorm or the final action sequences are incredibly riveting and enormous, it's the relationships in the book that are the most moving to me."

Fast fact . . .

In 2011, film makers Lionsgate held a worldwide competition in which five lucky winners were flown to the set of *The Hunger Games* to watch a scene being filmed and meet the cast!

Only the beginning . . .

Katniss realises that evil President Snow will one day punish her for her rebellious actions. Fortunately, the millions of fans desperately anticipating *The Hunger Games* movie won't have to wait long to see how – plans are already in place to film the second instalment, *Catching Fire*. So, happy Hunger Games! And may the odds be *ever* in your favour!

Designed by Simon Davis
Origination by Imagewrite Ltd
Printed and bound in Italy by Printer Trento

ISBN: 978 1 84812 233 8
1 3 5 7 9 10 8 6 4 2